The **Kodak** **Book** of

SCRAPBOOKING

PHOTOS of YOUR Children

D1314184

Combine one little boy with a wide-open deeryard and what do you get? A big messy lick to the face, also known as a deer kiss. This area at the zoo is amazing for kids. There is only one rule to abide by: only approach deer on the path. And today you met one loveable deer named Shadow. With the tolerance of a puppy, he let you hang on him (aka give hugs), tug on his fur (aka pet nicely) and stand nose to nose (aka give kisses). You were giddy with excitement when Shadow licked your face and went back for more. Only one problem: If your dog Audrey knew what was going on, she'd be jealous!

PITTSBURGH ZOO

9 9 05

Marla Kress

The **Kodak** **Book** of
SCRAPBOOKING
PHOTOS of YOUR Children

Kerry Arquette & Andrea Zocchi

Published by Lark Books
A Division of Sterling Publishing Co., Inc.
New York

Book Concept and Design: Cantata Books Inc. www.cantatabooks.com

Executive Editor: Kerry Arquette
Editor: Darlene D'Agostino
Copy Editor: Dena Twinem
Cover Design and Art Direction: Andrea Zocchi
Designer: Susha Roberts

Library of Congress Cataloging-in-Publication Data

Arquette, Kerry.
  The Kodak book of scrapbooking photos of your children : easy & fun techniques for beautiful scrapbook pages / Kerry Arquette & Andrea Zocchi. -- 1st ed.
     p. cm.
  Includes index.
  ISBN 1-57990-964-7 (pbk.)
  1. Photograph albums. 2. Photographs--Conservation and restoration. 3. Scrapbooks. 4. Photography of children. I. Zocchi, Andrea. II. Title.
   TR501.A7647 2007
   745.593--dc22
                              2006020564

10 9 8 7 6 5 4 3 2 1

First Edition

Published by Lark Books, A Division of Sterling Publishing Co., Inc.
387 Park Avenue South, New York, N.Y. 10016

© 2007, Eastman Kodak Company
Illustrations © Cantata Books Inc.

Distributed in Canada by Sterling Publishing,
c/o Canadian Manda Group, 165 Dufferin Street, Toronto, Ontario, Canada M6K 3H6

Distributed in the United Kingdom by GMC Distribution Services,
Castle Place, 166 High Street, Lewes, East Sussex, England BN7 1XU

Distributed in Australia by Capricorn Link (Australia) Pty Ltd., P.O. Box 704, Windsor, NSW 2756 Australia

Kodak and trade dress are trademarks of Kodak used by Lark Books under trademark license.

Kodak
LICENSED PRODUCT

If you have questions or comments about this book, please contact:
Lark Books
67 Broadway
Asheville, NC 28801
(828) 253-0467

Manufactured in China

ISBN 13: 978-1-57990-964-2
ISBN 10: 1-57990-964-7

For information about custom editions, special sales, premium and corporate purchases, please contact Sterling Special Sales Department at 800-805-5489 or specialsales@sterlingpub.com.

Table of Contents

Sonya Shaw

Scrapbooking Your Children!

GET THE KNOW-HOW NECESSARY TO CREATE FUN AND HEARTFELT PAGES ABOUT THE KIDS IN YOUR LIFE

When it comes to scrapbooking, there is no subject more irresistible than children. They are unfolding works of art. At one moment they are tiny, and the next day they seem to have grown a foot! And their moods, personalities and interests keep pace as they move from those oh-so-cute toddler clothes into scuffed-knee blue jeans and T-shirts. With such change taking place at such a frantic rate, it is almost impossible to remember the high points of your child's growth unless they are documented.

In this book, you'll learn what it takes to preserve the memories of your favorite children on scrapbook pages that are as creative as your little munchkin. You'll find basic scrapbooking terms and techniques as well as an introduction to the supplies you will need to get started.

Each and every page of this book is filled with inspirational art created by some of the most talented scrapbook artists around. Dive in to a world of scrapbooking you never dreamed existed, and begin crafting your own pages that you and your family are sure to cherish.

Samuel Cole

The Elements of a Successful Scrapbook Page

THE BASICS ARE BACK

While there are no "rules" when it comes to designing a scrapbook page, most artists agree that the majority of successful pages include a number of important features. Once you understand these elements, you can get creative with their presentation.

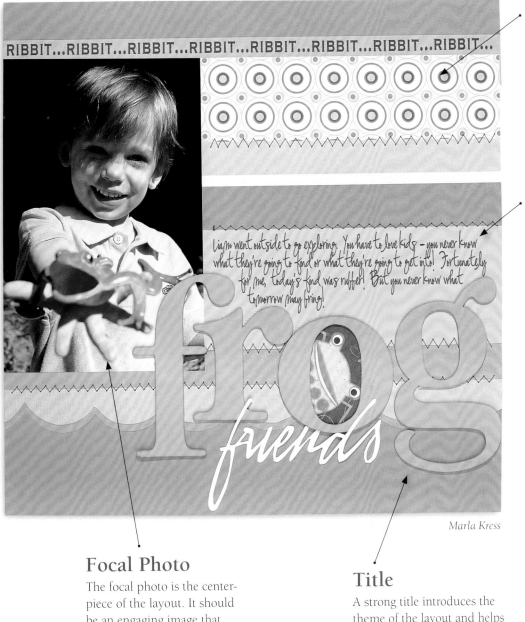

Marla Kress

Technique

Successful pages exhibit a creative technique, whether it's a simple mix of patterned paper or a classic color-blocked background.

Journaling

Journaling can be simple or elaborate. Its function is to tell the story and define the characters.

Focal Photo

The focal photo is the centerpiece of the layout. It should be an engaging image that draws immediate attention.

Title

A strong title introduces the theme of the layout and helps to unify the design.

Scrapbooking, Defined
EVERYTHING YOU NEED TO KNOW TO CREATE YOUR FIRST PAGE

If you're new to scrapbooking, it can be intimidating. There are so many terms! But, this handy-dandy list will make learning the basics easy as A-B-C. Also, use the 5-step guide to create a page and test your photo-storage IQ.

Samuel Cole

5 Steps to Creating a Scrapbook Page

1. select photos Choose the most compelling photo as the focal point and use the rest as support images. Crop as necessary.

2. write journaling Develop the theme of your page. Journaling can be short or long, just be sure to include it.

3. pick colors What emotion do you wish the page to convey? Choose colors to match the emotion. Convert photos to black-and-white, if necessary, to support the color scheme.

4. concept design Sketch a page design, making sure the page is balanced.

5. build your page Before you commit to adhesive, be sure you are happy with your design. When ready, mount your elements and enjoy!

Test Your Photo- and Negative-Storage IQ
See what you know and learn something new with this multiple-choice test

1. Photos and negatives should be stored
   a. together   b. separately   c. not at all
2. You should use _____ to store photos and negatives.
   a. plastic bags   b. a shoe box   c. photo-safe binders or boxes
3. Photos and negatives should be stored in what type of conditions?
   a. high humidity and lots of light b. fluctuating c. constant—not too humid, not too dry, not to hot, not too cool—and away from light
4. True or False: Glassine envelopes are safe homes for photos and negatives.
5. Storage and protection materials made of _____ are safe to use with photos.
   a. PVC   b. polyester   c. polypropylene   d. polyethylene   e. b, c & d

Answers: 1. b 2. c 3. c 4. False 5. e

Kay Rogers

Archival Terms to Know

Practice safe scrapbooking with the proper understanding of the following terms

Acid-free Materials with a pH of 7.0 or above. When shopping for materials for your scrapbook, look for acid-free items. Acids can react with photos, and acidic paper will yellow and become brittle over time. Keep in mind that the designation "acid-free" does not guarantee an item to be scrapbook safe.

Archival-quality A material that is safe for preservation purposes.

Buffer (to) To protect photos against potentially reactive elements or acid migration on a scrapbook page. Photos can be buffered with archival paper mats, which will create a barrier between photos and the rest of a scrapbook page.

De-acidification spray An alkaline spray that will help neutralize acids in paper items of questionable archival quality. Newspaper clippings can be treated with de-acidification spray to help stop the paper from yellowing or becoming brittle.

Lignin-free A paper material free of lignin, the binding agent in plants that give them strength. Papers and photo papers with lignin will deteriorate and yellow over time.

Page protector Clear plastic sleeve that fits over a finished scrapbook page and into an album to protect the page from outside elements.

Photo-safe Term designating a material that will not chemically react with photographs.

Pigment ink Permanent ink that is of archival quality—it is acid-free and lightfast, meaning it will not fade when exposed to natural or artificial light.

PVC polyvinyl chloride. Plastic that is not safe to use in conjunction with your scrapbooks or photo storage. Commonly referred to as "vinyl," it emits a strong odor and may release highly corrosive gases that will harm your scrapbooks and photos.

Scrapbooking Supplies

A SCRAPBOOKER NEEDS THE RIGHT TOOLS FOR PROPER CROPPING

When your child sets out for his first day of school, no doubt he is properly prepared with all of the necessary supplies. Paper? Check. Paste? Check. Binder? Check. To crop, just like in school, you need to be prepared with the right tools and supplies. The tools and supplies on this page are must-haves for all scrapbookers. From buying the perfect adhesive to learning about all the different cutting tools, here is everything you need to know to get started scrapbooking properly.

Albums

Your child's school binder (hopefully) keeps him organized by subject. A scrapbook album has a similar function. Albums serve to protect and organize your scrapbook pages. There are all types of styles and sizes of albums, not to mention binding mechanisms, and there are pros and cons associated with each. No matter what album you choose, be sure it is of archival quality. Materials used to construct the album should be acid-, lignin- and PVC-free.

Adhesive

Choosing the correct adhesive for your scrapbook is more complicated than selecting school paste or glue for your child. Although there are a lot of choices, the one you select most often boils down to preference. Do you prefer working with wet or dry glue? Do you like the convenience of roll-on adhesive? In the beginning, it's best to pick up a few different types of adhesives to help you tackle a variety of jobs. Purchase a glue pen for detail work, an all-purpose tape runner and a bottle of wet adhesive for tougher jobs. Adhesives should be scrapbook- and photo-safe.

Colorants

Scrapbooking colorants may not carry the carefree charm of, say, finger paints, but having a wide and creative selection instead is worth it. Scrapbookers have been known to employ acrylic paint, inks, colored pencils, chalks, pens and more to bring pages to life with color.

Cutting tools

The most basic cutting tool for scrapbookers is the craft knife. It comes in handy for all types of cutting situations. It's also an excellent idea to have a dedicated pair of scissors for cutting paper (if you're into fabric, get another pair for those jobs). Paper trimmers will help you make nice, long cuts. Round out your arsenal with decorative-edged scissors, punches, nested cutting templates and a circle cutter.

Embellishments

Fibers! Beads! Charms! Die cuts! Stickers! Brads! Eyelets! Frames! Oh my gosh, the list goes on and on. This is the stuff that makes scrapbooking so much fun! These are items that both you and your kids will appreciate. Heck, you might even fight over them. But not to worry, there are enough embellishments in every shape, every size, every theme and every color to go around.

Hello World! This is ME!

From the moment they arrive in this world, babies show glimmers of their own very individual personalities. As the child grows, so does her character. That sense of humor, the temper, the moods, intelligence and all of the other traits she carries inside seem to fill her small frame until they burst free—to the delight of those around her.

The best photos of children are those that are unposed. Rather than stretching a cheesy smile across their faces, they are spontaneously interacting and reacting to the world around them. Their personalities are on display and, if you are lucky enough to capture an honest moment on film, it can result in a spectacular scrapbook page that screams, "This is ME!"

the world laughs with you

CADIE

Lisa Risser

I'm Happy

I HAVE A SMILE A MILE WIDE

Remember your baby's first smile? It made your heart lurch, and you called out to everyone within hearing distance to come witness the miracle. Now that your child has left infancy behind, the smiles are even broader. The joy you feel when you see one remains the same. Capture your child's grins in photos that show not only those sparkling pearly whites, but humor as well.

Monica Coffman

A

What a grin! You just have to smile back at this young beauty. Patterned papers embrace a terrific black-and-white photo. The title letter is a monogram rub-on. Rub-ons form the minimal journaling on blocks of colored papers.

Summer 2005 Jace age 6

Haircut

Handmade flash cards make the creation of this little-guy page quick and easy. A patterned-paper background is layered with a strip of coordinating paper. Minimal journaling and an oversized photo of the model complete the page.

Jill Utrup

Happy Girl

This little diva has a lot to be happy about. She's scrapbooked on a pretty pink page that complements those too-cool pink glasses. The large monogram is cut from green paper and contains a stitched edge. The artist also stitched large circles on the pink floral patterned paper to embellish.

Create Your Own Monogram
Large letters are all the rage and easy to create

Fonts Choose a font and type letter in a large point size (400 - 600). Print in reverse onto the back of patterned paper and cut out.

Die cuts Use an oversized die-cut or chipboard letter as a tracing guide. Put the letter facedown onto the back of patterned paper, trace and cut out.

Johanna Peterson

I'm Sweet

INNOCENT AND ADORABLE

The sweet innocence of your child melts you each time you are gifted with another wilted dandelion bouquet. She hands it over confidently, knowing that you will react with appropriate pleasure. And your pleasure is hers. That same sweetness is pooled in her eyes in quiet moments of contemplation or solo play. Scrapbook photos of your child's sweet nature on gentle pages that focus on those mesmerizing, trusting eyes.

Sweetness

What is inspiring the fantastic expression on this little cupid's face? That's for her to know! The photo capturing her moment of delight is for us to enjoy. It is mounted on a background of sweetly stitched papers. An oversized stamped title, tiny flowers strung on a delicate piece of fiber, a journaled bookplate and sticker complete the page.

Rebekah Robinson

Precious Boy

This digital page calls on piles of decorative digital papers to draw the eye to the so-sweet photo of the little boy. Stitching and brads are created digitally as well. The poetic journaling block was discovered on a scrapbooking Web site.

Make the Most of Your Photos

Surround your photo with meaningful journaling and intimately connect the photo to a meaningful sentiment. Words can be handwritten, typed, stamped or created with rub-ons or stickers.

She

She is everything a mother could hope for in a daughter. The artist who created this page makes that clear through hand journaling that surrounds the photo. A stamped title occupies a prominent position on the photo mat, which in turn is mounted on a background of terrific patterned papers.

I'm Complex

IT WILL TAKE US A LIFETIME TO KNOW EACH OTHER

Your child is complex. While you may have glimmers of what goes on inside that miniature head, chances are there are thoughts and feelings you can't possibly imagine. The many sides of your child are part of the miracle of life. Do your best to honor your child's many facets on pages that speak more loudly than words.

Martha Crowther

100% Authentic

Whether beseeching, giggling wickedly or participating in a quiet moment, this beautiful boy is uncompromisingly himself. His mother's journaling details the pride she takes in that. The focal image is balanced with a row of support photos that share a single mat. Rub-ons create the title and add balance to the layout.

Blue (blu) 1. sad 2. low in spirits 3. gloomy

Blue (blu) 1. sad 2. low in spirits 3. gloomy

ANNIE b.
2005

Linda Garrity

Blue Girl

What's there to be so blue about, Child? That furry hat and fluffy coat are sure to keep you warm! Oh well, this wonderful page is sure to coax a smile from everyone who sees it. The image is triple matted and bordered with a collection of ribbons. The title block forms a page border while definitions border the photo on two other sides.

Rocker

Cute and adorable boy or wild and dangerous rock star? This artist feels that her nephew dons a rock-star appearance when he wears his knit skull cap, so she let the photo dictate the wild page design. The doodled background is actually patterned paper. She hand journaled to match the line quality of the paper and cut the journaling into captions that also serve to direct the reader's eye to the photo.

Intensity. Depth.

It's in his blood...

It's Inevitable. Sean

Aaron Hyde.

rockER

Jen Jockisch

I'm Silly

LOOK AT THIS FACE, MOM!

It's called "pulling a face," and nobody's better at it than kids. They take those perfect little features and drag and draw them into cartoonlike images. They are intentionally being funny, and that's what makes the antics so perfect. Before you know it, their sense of humor will morph, and you'll leave these silly moments behind. Snap those photos today!

Goofy Boy

This young man measures up to the highest silly standard possible. The measuring tape embellishment cuts across the photo, driving home its point. A letter sticker title reinforces the concept. Layered patterned papers on top of a textured cardstock background form the perfect palette for the photo. Stitching and distressing make this page the genuine article.

Share Smith-Baxter

Annie B

Two photos of this cute clown are matted and mounted on a yellow crackle-patterned background. A flutter of ribbon serves as photo corners for the primary image while a large flower embellishes the support photo. Journaling is printed on a transparency. Acrylic paint is used to highlight portions of the text. The paint is applied on the back of the transparency so as not to cover up the text.

Linda Garrity

Be You

Squish it, pull it, mash it. That's what faces are for, right? Just ask this boy. He's having a terrific time just goofing around. The primary image is mounted on a patterned paper background. Large paper monogram letters are combined to create the title, while rub-ons are used to journal. The supporting image is showcased within a sleek metal frame.

Make the Most of Your Photos

Silly doesn't always happen on demand. To coax laughter and carefree funny faces from your child, get into the act yourself. Silliness is an art that most photographers spend lifetimes trying to master.

Charlene Walberg

I'm Spunky

WANNA KNOW WHAT I'M THINKING?

You never know what's going to come out of the mouths of spunky children. You can count on the fact that they are going to speak their minds. You can see it in their faces. Photos that feature your child in his best spunky form are full of character. Scrapbook them on whimsical pages that push the boundaries with design, pattern and color.

Julie Detlef

Spunky

Creatively cut patterned papers resembling a flower act as a mat for this terrific ribbon-wrapped photo. Stamps are used to create the title. Additional journaling appears around the edges of the photo mat, and a quote is lettered on top of the individual title letters.

Make the Most of Your Photos

Journaling can add more than just the facts to a scrapbook page. Take a moment to really describe the events surrounding your photo and you'll find that the memories remain much clearer for much longer. This artist writes, "Sydnee is truly a spunky little girl. This day she was lovin' her groovy glasses…She was actually climbing on a mulch pile while she was trying to be a girly girl…just no hope. She makes every situation fun. I wouldn't change anything about her."

Silly Little Man

Sometimes the world seems topsy-turvy…
especially when you're a very little guy. The
image of this boy exploring the many sides
of life is scrapbooked on pale orange cardstock and two different patterned papers.
The journaling block, below the chipboard
title, describes a mother's joy in her son's
sense of humor.

silly little man

You are so silly! A funny little man! You just love to get a laugh out of us,
no matter what the circumstance or consequence. You kept doing this on
the beach and we were laughing so hard. The look of delight on your
face tells all. Of course, you weren't too happy when we had to scrub
your hair that evening to get all the sand out. My Silly Little Man!

Celeste Smith

You-er Than You

Brilliant sun yellow and sky blue
papers set a joyful mood for this page.
The papers are layered to support
the matted photo of this saucy little
guy (that expression says that he's a
mini man who's full of personality). A
die-cut tag and ribbon embellish the
layout. The artist created the look of
faux stitching by detailing the edges of
the blue paper with pen slashes.

Peggy Severins

I'm All Girl

I LOVE RIBBONS AND LACE

Little girls and ribbons. Little girls and flowers! Little girls and pastel colors! They are all marriages made in heaven. Even tomboys look their best when surrounded by gentle blues, pinks, mauves and creams. So scrapbook photos of your daughter's girly traits on pages that are sprinkled with charm.

Shelly Boyd

Charmed

We are charmed by the delicate details of this layout. The background is formed with layer upon layer of coordinating patterned papers. L-shaped portions of gingham paper form corners around the photo. Blocks of paper are strung together with ribbon to display rub-on journaling concepts. Rub-ons and bows embellish the page. Cross-stitching is perfectly executed to create a border around two sides of the layout.

Katie Watson

Bloom Where You Are Planted

This page recalls the comfort of a favorite quilt. In fact, stitch marks are drawn around each of the flower embellishments to further the quilt theme. Stickers form the page title, and a delicate blue ribbon completes the picture.

Make the Most of Your Photos

Give your photo a graceful circular shape by cropping it. Use a pot or pan or another circular household supply to help you outline the circle. Lightly sketch the shape on the back of your photo before cutting it to form.

Flower Girl

You may have to be a master seamstress to sew a flower girl outfit, but with even the most elementary skills, you can stitch together papers to create a charming scrapbook-page background. Cardstock stickers embellish the bottom of the page, and a stamped design forms page borders on either side of the photo. Add a bouquet of flowers for a feminine touch.

Karen Buck

All That Sugar and Spice!

HOW TO INCLUDE GIRLY KEEPSAKES ON SCRAPBOOK PAGES

What would life be like without little girls? B-O-R-I-N-G! Moms, aunts, grandmas the world over would sigh with despair that they had nobody to dress in frilly outfits. There would be no cute little bottoms to cover in lacy-butt panties.

Luckily, the world has an unending supply of mini femmes. If you have such a sweet pea in your own life, get giddy about all of the fun flourishes you can add to little-girl scrapbook pages. Use portions of her beloved-but-outgrown clothes and toy accents that hold special memories.

Feminine Fabric

From bedding to stuffed animals, this young model loves chenille fabric. The "soft, nubby, warm, cozy, pretty, old-fashioned, comforting, snuggly" fabric characteristics are shared by the little girl. The model is posed snuggling a bear among a backdrop of pastel chenille pillows. Snipped pieces of fabric from bedding are attached to the layout with staples, stitching and brads.

Angie Head

Cherish It Always

Girl ephemera and keepsakes to save forever

Stop! Before you send those old clothes to the church charity sale and before you say goodbye to those berets that held baby-fine hair, ask yourself, "Can I use these on my scrapbook pages?" Here are some wonderful items for your girly-girl pages:

- Clothing tags
- Berets
- Dress-up jewelry
- Doll clothes
- Clothing patches
- Brownie and Girl Scout pins and patches

- ID tag from the "Going to Grandmas" luggage set
- Belt buckles
- Patterned shoe laces
- Swatches from favorite clothing
- Stickers from the sticker collection
- Smocked portions of dresses

Accessory Pieces

It's not the clothes that make the outfit, it's the accessories. This page details the artist's indulgence in buying cute winter hats for her daughter, despite the fact that the family lives in Houston, Texas! The hat will be too small by next year, so the artist eventually snipped off the bloom of flowers at the hat's crown and used them to texturize this page. The artist glued the flowers to the background, but accents such as this could also be stitched or applied with foam adhesive.

Angie Head

Jodi Heinen

Clothing Swatches

One of the best things about having a little girl in your life is her adorable wardrobe. From fancy and frilly to down-home and denim, show your girl's style on a scrapbook page. On this page, the artist pays homage to her daughter's casual chic. She includes the pocket from a pair of outgrown blue jeans.

27

I'm All Boy
GOT A SNIP OR A SNAIL?

Give me a ball, and take away my shoes. Give me a bike, and take away my shirt. Give me a chance, and I'll show you what a bundle of energy looks like! Scrapbook photos of your boy on pages that look like they've lived a little. Distressing, tearing, stitching and chalking papers lends a very "boy" feeling to your layouts.

Laura Bailey

He Has Impeccable Style

Freedom! That's what a boy's life is all about—freedom of movement, of expression and (in this case) freedom from a shirt and shoes. Faux sticker stitches give this page a homey feel. Patterned papers join a collection of stickers to make up this page. No fuss. No muss. No problem.

Robyn Lantz

Thank You

Boys are anything but orderly, and this page artfully captures the sense of the subject. Ripped pieces of patterned paper blocks are mounted onto a cardstock background. Photo turns decorate the corners of the image. Sticker letters create the title, and journaling snakes around the edges of the page and says, "thank you—for your weed bouquets, your gifts of smoothy rocks, all the art you make for me..."

Freedom

This young patriot knows how lucky he is to be living in the "land of the free and the home of the brave." The photo of his enthusiastic celebration is scrapbooked on a waving block of textured blue cardstock. The journaling block flows along the same curving lines while the sticker page-title creates a sweeping vertical line between them.

Make the Most of Your Photos

When cropping photos, consider cropping a photo into a vertical panoramic. The narrow width focuses the reader's attention on the subject.

Linda Harrison

Trophies, Trucks and T-Rexes
HOW TO INCLUDE BOYISH KEEPSAKES ON SCRAPBOOK PAGES

Boys! Despite the fact that they have tendencies to leave baseball gloves, tiny toy cars, skateboards, string, pebbles and paper clips in their wake, we simply couldn't do without them!

Watching a son grow up fills parents with a sense of both pride and loss. By scrapbooking his toys and creations you'll always be able to hold on to memories of the times when your mini man was still small enough to crawl up into your lap for cuddles.

Drawn Favorites

A piece of scrap paper and a set of crayons can keep many children busy for hours. This little guy's life revolves around his fascination with dinosaurs. The artist found a rendering of a T. Rex created by her son and cut it from the paper it was drawn on. After treating the image with de-acidification spray, she attached it to the layout.

Sheila Doherty

Cherish It Always
Boy ephemera and keepsakes to save forever

Yes, these things may be dirty and worn, but they will forever remind you that this boy, who one day will become a man, was once indeed a child. Here are some items to include on your scrapbook pages that will make you say, "boy, oh boy!"

- Trading cards
- Stickers
- Belt buckles
- Pieces of worn blue jeans
- Sports emblems
- Swatches from team-sports uniforms
- Snippets of footballs, soccer balls, baseballs, etc.
- Paper crowns
- Parts from toy cars
- Action-figure outfits
- Scanned covers from books and books-on-tape
- Comic books
- CD liner notes
- Scans of awards or photos of trophies

Boy Toys

Rollin', rollin', rollin', keep those pages rollin'! Tiny toy tires are wonderful to use as accents on your scrapbook pages about boys and their toys. (A bit of warning: Be sure you don't remove tires from his favorite toys!) This page captures a boy hard at play in a sandbox. The photo shows stern determination as he maneuvers a toy dump truck. The journaling block features a set of toy tires that thematically supports the layout and draws attention to the journaling block.

Sheila Doherty

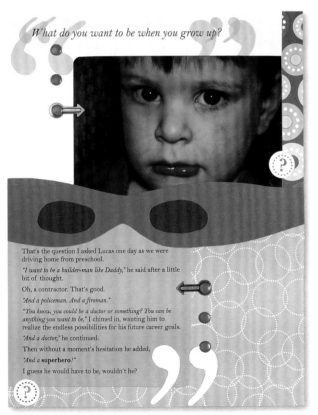

Sheila Doherty

Superhero Masks

Some boys want to be policemen or firemen when they grow up. Some want to follow in the footsteps of their fathers. Yet others want to be doctors. This boy wants to be all of that and more—his major ambition is to be a superhero. This page is based on a conversation the artist had with her son. It details his wild career ambitions. She stretched a paper superhero mask across the middle of the layout to support the page theme and add spunk and color to the design.

31

My Name Is...

A ROSE BY ANY OTHER NAME

You struggle for months and sift through endless numbers of baby name books before you decide on the perfect name for your child. Why not create a scrapbook page featuring your final selection? Use the name to create the page title, or be more subtle and include it as an element within a photo.

Charrie Shockey

What's in a Name?

A rose by any other name should just try to be as sweet as this page! The title blocks are lifted slightly off the polka-dot background with foam adhesive. Red inked stencil letters spell out "name," and tiny star shapes are punched in the corners of the paper. A tidy journaling block tells the story behind the page.

Make the Most of Your Photos

A photo mat does not always have to be square. In fact, it can be any shape you wish. Consider playing off of a pattern in your background paper. Cut or punch shapes similar to the pattern. Layer them under your photo for a cohesive look.

Michelle Oatman
Photo: Melanie Vale

Silhouette Cropping

Cutting around the edges of an image is a perfect way to draw attention to the subject. Here are some guidelines for best results.

- Never ever, ever, ever, ever cut one-of-a-kind photos! What you consider "extra" portions of the photo may later offer detail and context that will be of tremendous interest.

- When silhouette cropping an image, use very sharp scissors. Cut cleanly around the outside of the subject you wish to feature.

- When mounting the cropped photo, make sure the lower edge of the image is "grounded." In other words, don't place the image in the center of your scrapbook page because the image will look like a paper doll set down on a table top. Give your cropped picture something to stand on, or set it along your lower page border.

Talisyn

Handcut title letters are matted with darker paper to help them pop off of this flowered background paper. The model is surrounded by tiny flowers, bringing a three-dimensional effect to the layout.

Oh So Sarah

Cardstock, patterned paper and stickers are used to create this colorful page. A concise journaling block describes a young lady who has a solid sense of her own fashion style even at this early age.

Teresa Olier

33

They Call Me...

ALL BOY, ALWAYS

Whether you named your son after a well-loved grandfather, or were drawn to one of the hip new names of our times, he has made it uniquely his own. Scrapbook your special guy on pages that brag about his title!

Stacey Bogert

Nathan Today

TROUBLE! But the kind of trouble that you want to kiss and hug and feature on his own scrapbook page. Textured cardstock forms the background for this layout. A circular theme is carried forward by cropping both photos into circles, journaling around the circle edges and mounting the large die-cut letters in a curved pattern. Brads, ribbon and stickers bring whimsy to the page.

Cutting Corners (and Circles) Perfectly

A circle cutter is the perfect way to safely cut circles for frames, embellishments or to crop images. But if you have the urge to cut and you have no special tool for it, use anything round you have at hand, such as…pots and pans, Sit 'n' Spin, plates, cups and glasses, jar lid or can, hockey puck, coaster; it just has to be round.

Dimples

Young Matthew has dimples that could make a girl giddy. Adding to his charm is his appearance of shyness. Both those qualities are featured in this super photo. The monogrammed "M" joins jigsaw letters to create the title. A bit of ribbon and a three-dimensional flower embellish the layout.

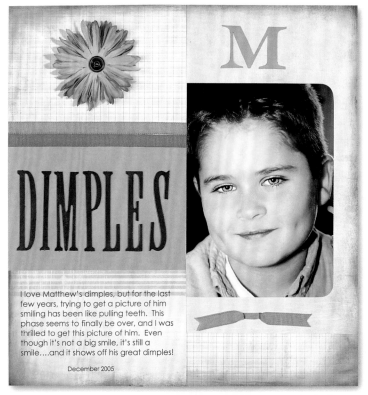

Linda Garrity

Amy Vaughan

Dathan at 12

Even rough and tough boys have a gentle side, and this photo perfectly captures one of those sweeter moments. The photo is mounted on a pattern-blocked background. A hidden journaling block is tucked behind the photo and details the boy's first stages of adolescence.

I'm Hard to Pin Down

JUST TRY TO DEFINE ME

Children's likes and dislikes change as often as their moods. Journal about specific things about which your child has voiced an opinion. Include favorites and pet peeves, character traits, vocabulary quirks and more. For fun, ask your child to actually do the writing himself. Include his handwritten thoughts on your page.

Kim Moreno

You

A large block of patterned paper creates a playful mood for an all-boy photo. Title letters are created with oversized stickers. The stitched line under the title is repeated with stitching around the large L-shaped photo corners.

Shop 'til You Drop at Your Local Fabric Store

Hobby and craft stores are stocked with supplies for eager scrapbookers. But, let your eye wander and you may find additional supplies at your local fabric store that will set your creativity free.

- Fabric for textured page backgrounds or embellishments
- Thread for stitching patterns or securing elements to your page
- Zippers for creative page designs
- Snaps, buttons, hooks and eyes for embellishments
- Lace, ribbon and fibers
- Patches
- Fabric dye

Girl

A sprinkling of brads secures slender journaling strips to the background page on this layout. The journaling describes this young girl's favorites, including her favorite movie ("Cinderella Story"), favorite sports (volleyball and horseback riding) and favorite song ("So Yester-day"). Tiny bows are tied through eyelets along the edge of the photo and around the monogram. Rub-on words wrap the layout in sentiment.

Shuri Orr

Taylor

The craggy texture of the tree trunk seen in the photo is supported by distressed journaling slips and stamped and inked title blocks. Sturdy staples hold elements to the background. Strips of ribbon soften the page.

Sandra Liddell

37

Lessons Learned

A SCRAPBOOK-PAGE MAKEOVER TEACHES DESIGN UNITY

The layout below features a photo of an exuberant boy. "I created 'My Graham Cracker' in January 2004," says Samuel Cole. "My nephew's middle name is Graham and, because he such a little ball of energy, I call him my 'Graham Cracker.' In the layout, I wanted to show his playful, fun, energetic personality."

But the resulting layout is a bit disjointed. While Samuel had a clear theme in mind, his choice of colors, accents, page title and journaling did not work together to support the theme. Looking at the layout now, Samuel says: "Overall, it's just plain bad. There's not a whole lot that I like about the layout, except for the sweet, fun pictures of Thomas."

On the right, Samuel re-created the layout. The overhaul shows definite improvement. Because of the changes made, the page is completely unified in regard to theme, and the eye travels effortlessly around the layout.

GOOD, BUT...

Firecracker elements seem odd and a bit clumsy. They also look outdated.

The journaling does not support the title, leaving the reader to wonder why the artist refers to the boy as his "graham cracker."

The interactive element, while helpful to house more photos, is jarring because of disjointed photo crops.

Page lacks a strong color scheme. The chosen patterned paper does not make photos pop.

Samuel Cole

The colors and patterns in the papers are more energetic. The muted tones help pop the bright blue of the model's shirt.

The page theme is unified, from the title and the journaling to the colors and the accents. The journaling supports the title, and the word accents reinforce the theme as well.

The focal photo was reduced to 5 x 7" so as not to overpower the layout. This helped the overall balance and also allowed the support photos to shine.

The interactive element was removed in favor of showing the support photos, which allows the reader to truly see the model's personality.

Samuel Cole

Be a Better Scrapbooker

3 Tips from Samuel Cole on how to develop your scrapbook style:

Use patterned paper to maximum effect. Mixed correctly, patterned papers can put the "pow" in "powerful" layout design.

Never let embellishments overwhelm the photos. Ask yourself if you have chosen the proper balance, tone and color.

Use what you love. Don't feel pressured to use trendy products or techniques if they don't feel natural to you.

A Day in My Life

They are here one moment and over there the next. On the go in shorts and a T-shirt only to be replaced an hour later by a swimsuit, team uniform or tree-climbing blue jeans and yet a new T-shirt. Children's days are FILLED with activity.

Scrapbooking photos of your child's day is almost as much fun as watching him play. Because the range of activities varies so widely, you have unlimited reasons to experiment with different palettes, theme papers and activities. Others will enjoy viewing these pages of a day in the life of your little whirlwind.

With each leaf a miracle — walt whitman

CRISP

Whatever the SEASON you are my miracle

a leaf

Debbie VanMarter

Beach Fun!

SAND, SURF AND SUNSCREEN

Grab those swimsuits, the beach towel, the SPF 45 and lots of film! You're going to want to photograph your child's romp in the sand. Scrapbook photos of brightly colored swim outfits, towels and umbrellas on hot pages that make you wish you were a child again.

Miranda Ferski

Play With Abandon

It's not exactly a yellow polka-dot bikini, but it is teeny weeny enough to fit this little beach bum. The patterned papers forming the page background draw their colors directly from the swimsuit print. Hot-colored floral stickers reflect the swimsuit's pattern. The paper title letters also serve as a page border, embracing the high energy photo.

Hot and Cool Colors

Select colors for your pages that produce the desired mood.

Red, orange, yellow and hot pink steam things up, actually making the heart race faster. Use them to energize your scrapbook pages.

Blue, green and some purples cool things down. In fact, studies show that racehorses that are placed in green stalls after they run cool down faster than expected. Use these colors for laid-back pages.

Using Line and Shape in Design
Identify the line quality in your photos for an inspired design

Your scrapbook page design should echo elements in your photos. For example, when deciding whether to use straight or curvy lines, let your photos be the judge. In "Beauty on the Beach," the artist chose to use wavy lines because they
resemble the rolling mounds of sand on which her daughter is playing. The same with shape—if you see circle shapes in your photos, pull the shape into your design.

Beauty on the Beach

Patterned paper, cut to form ocean waves, laps against the photo of this mermaid. The photo mat and title block are hot orange, and delicate beach flowers in shades of peppery pink embellish the layout. The title is created with chipboard and plastic letter stickers.

Jennifer Santos-Hamer
Photo: Robert Hamer

St. George Island, July 2004

Beach Fun

Sand on the nose and sand in the toes— that's what this little darling is all about! The photo showing her beachy day is scrapbooked on layers of textured papers. The terrific title is pieced together with decorative metal letter discs mounted on square paper blocks. A journaled transparency creates a border along the left side of the layout.

Jane Bohn

43

Park Fun!
SWING, SLIDE AND SPIN

Whether upside down or right side up, kids love outings to the park. Excursions to these playgrounds offer able opportunity for action photos. Select your palette by drawing colors from your child's outfit or the play equipment, or reach for patterned papers that scream "playful." Snip, stitch and scrapbook your own way to fun.

Monkey Girl

This little girl is a charmer, and her enthusiasm is contagious. Gentle purple patterned papers recede a bit, allowing the photos to move forward visually. The groupings of tiny flowers decorate page and photo corners. Ribbons strung horizontally across the page defy the vertical stripes in the patterned paper below. The artist journals, "You're never too old to be a monkey on the playground. I never get tired of watching you play."

Lisa Turley

Capturing Action Photos

When you are photographing kids in motion you need to be prepared. Consider the following:

- Focus your camera on the spot where your child is most likely to pass.
- Rather than trying to track your child through your viewfinder, allow your child to enter your sights and then snap the photo.
- Anticipate the moment you will need to snap the photo.
- Take more photos than you think you will need to scrapbook the event. (Chances are some will be blurry and you may entirely miss your subject in a few frames.)
- Use a faster speed film to capture quick movement.
- Be sure there is enough light—action shots require faster film, which requires more light to properly expose and image.

Lisa Dorsey

All Wound Up

Remember when a ride on a twisted swing didn't leave your stomach in knots? This series of photos helps bring back those childhood moments vividly. The focal image is mounted directly on the clean white background. Supporting photos are matted on pink paper before being mounted on a wavy stretch of wild patterned paper. Both the title and journaling ride the perimeters of the wave.

Swing Into Spring

Broad strips of colored and patterned papers create a quick and easy background for this oversized photo. The tidy title and journaling are created with a computer and printed on the colorful paper. The flower embellishment is made by cutting and assembling circles cut from spare patterned paper.

Contrasting Line and Shape in Design
Use contrast to add energy to a design

For design inspiration, look to the photos. After you have identified line qualities and shapes to mimic, consider adding contrast. Contrast will add energy and movement to a layout. For example, in "All Wound Up," the artist based the curving lines of the design and picked patterned paper that featured circles to symbolize a smooth swinging movement. She then added a series of square-cropped photos to contrast against the curvy shapes. The contrast is subtle because she rounded the square corners to match the curves that are inherent to her design.

Heather Dewaelsche

Pretend Fun!

DRESS-UP AND MAKE-BELIEVE

What a delight it is to watch a child play dress-up. She puts on that tiara, or he puts on that war paint or that goofy hat, and becomes so immersed in pretend that the "real world" disappears. It is magic in its most childlike form. Scrapbook photos of your child's dress-up play and enjoy the insights she provides into the imagination behind that downy hair and gap-toothed grin.

Beth Root

Finding Colorants in a Pinch

Out of colorants? Try these household supplies.

If you want to colorize portions of your page but don't have a scrapbook colorant in your supply box, consider getting creative with moist tea bags, walnut extract, eye shadow, eyeliner, lipstick and blush, crayons as well as other household items. Note that these are not necessarily photo-safe, so separate your images from colorants with mats.

Dreamer

Sometimes dreams take place at night and sometimes we play them out in the light of day. This...this...wild thing embraces the moment, easily holding his place on a page of mixed patterned papers. Rub-on words adorn three ribbon-strung tags. Embellished circles balance the page nicely.

Make the Most of Your Photos

Who doesn't love photographing her child playing outdoors? Capturing a good image can be tricky, though, because of bright sunlight. If outside and camera-ready during bright, afternoon sun, find a shady spot and ask your child to pose. The filtered light will result in images without harsh shadows.

Adorable

Everybody go ahead and coo. This little lion is worth making a fuss over. The precious photo is scrapbooked on a page of red, white and black papers. The journaling is as creative as the costume.

DeAnna Heidmann

Lily Goldsmith

Shining Star

What a little princess! This photo of her luxurious locks and shining crown is scrapbooked on layered patterned papers. The title is a mix of stamped and distressed chipboard letters. Journaling blocks, below, tell of the benefits of being a girl and detail the special traits of the model. The page is embellished with playful feminine flowers.

Helping Out Fun!
SWEEPING UP, WASHING UP AND COOKIN' UP

It is said that if a child can do a job, he should do a job. Helping with the household chores gives your child a sense of confidence and an understanding that he is an important contributing member of the family. Scrapbook photos of your child's work efforts with photos that will fill him with pride, and you with awe in his giving spirit.

Helping Daddy

Yard chores are hard work, especially when the shovel is twice as tall as you are! But that doesn't seem to faze this little gardener. Photos of her efforts to help out are scrapbooked side by side. Blocks of patterned papers are puzzle-pieced together to form the lower portion of the page. Journaling strips, stitching, an index tab and stickers complement the theme and palette.

Maria Burke

Make the Most of Your Photos
Want to stitch on a page but are afraid that your efforts might result in wavering lines and a bit of knotting? That rustic stitched look fits in perfectly on pages with outdoorsy photos or those that call for a more earthy look. So go for it!

ILona Havenaar-Wise

Household Help

Pitching in around the house is a big step for a little guy. This photo celebrates his achievement. The digitally created page boasts a thoughtful journaling block recounting the artist's surprise to see her 6-year-old happily washing dishes.

My Little Chef

A bit of salt, a bit of pepper and just the right hat and apron are the keys to successful cooking. This little chef has the recipe down pat. Three photos of her working are scrapbooked on patterned papers. Tiny flowers, shiny brads and a ribbon make the layout especially appetizing. The title is composed of a mix of lettering styles. The words start small and end large to emphasize the word "chef."

Anita Ford

School Fun!

READING, WRITING AND 'RITHMETIC

Learning is fun, and children who learn THAT at an early age are most likely going to do well at their studies. Make a point of telling your child about your own school adventures as you scrapbook her school fun. These school-themed pages are a wonderful way to track your child's yearly growth.

Must Be Red

Back-to-school shopping? Nevermind the school uniform, the sweaters and blue jeans or spiffy new shoes! Focus instead on the supplies this young student has—every piece in her academic ensemble is cherry red! Photos are scrapbooked on—what else?!—red patterned papers. Creative journaling shares the youngster's fashion insights: "Red is the new pink (which used to be the new black)."

Maria Gallardo-Williams

School-Photo Checklist

School photos can include much more than just formal portraits and class pictures. When creating school-themed pages, consider scrapbooking the following:

- Photos and receipts from back-to-school shopping trips
- Photos and packaging from newly assembled school supplies
- Photos of before and after the first day of school. Scrapbook conversations about your child's emotions.
- Photos of bus-stop antics, the bus and bus driver
- Photos of your child's classmates, teacher and activities
- School art and papers as well as report cards and student directories

Me and My Backpack

It's a big day for this little gal! She's off to school with a backpack full of excitement. The photos of her are mounted on a background of red cardstock and layered patterned papers. The curved lines of the papers provide an "over the hills" feeling of movement to the page. Letter stickers, transparencies and a frame join a circular journaling block to complete the layout.

Lily Goldsmith

Homework

It all begins with a series of squiggles and somewhere along the line those arbitrary lines become letters and words and sentences and before you know it...you've got a young author! Photos of this little guy's first efforts are showcased on this layout. A series of supporting photos at the bottom of the page create a sense of growth and movement.

Nicole Stark

Music Fun!

HORNS, SONGS AND PRACTICE...MUSIC

Take a deep breath and think about the future. Listening to those hours of "Mary Had a Little Lamb" plunked out on your child's new instrument will pay off when he is entertaining you with Mozart! Even if your child decides to set aside his musical instrument in the future, he'll carry an understanding of the discipline music requires. Scrapbook pages of his early musical enthusiasm to remind him where and when the seeds were planted.

Marla Kress

Playlist

Can you name your favorite songs? This little guy can (and chances are that he knows all the lyrics as well!). This well-journaled page includes two separate journaling blocks. One lists the boy's favorite songs and performers and the other is a narrative written by the artist describing her son's love of music. Journaling blocks are separated by carefully cut pieces of patterned paper and a sticker title. A large monogram "S" forms the first letter in the phrase "Singer/songwriter."

Include Your Handwriting

There are a great number of ways to journal on a scrapbook page. Handwritten journaling adds a very personal touch to a piece of artwork. As experts have documented, handwriting is unique to every individual and tells a lot about his personality and the period in which he lived. In years to come, your handwritten journaling will be of tremendous interest to your descendants. What about the "messies" (wavering lines, uneven spacing, misspelled words, etc.)? Don't worry. Any busy mother reading your text in years to come will understand that keeping up with a youngster doesn't always allow time for perfect penmanship.

Irish Rap

From her gleaming long hair to her high arches and appealing expression, this young dancer looks like she's got what it takes to get the audiences on their feet. The three photos are scrapbooked on earth-tone papers. Chipboard letters and specialty papers are punched into circles to create the title. A tag, adorned with a die cut and decorative stick pin, add flourish to the upper portion of the page. A bookplate and date appear in the lower right corner.

Make the Most of Your Photos

Avoid height distortion when photographing a standing model by holding the camera level with the model's waist.

Maria Gallardo-Williams

Music

This young clarinet player is featured on a creative page of wildflower patterned paper. Lines created with a ruler are drawn across the top of the page to mimic sheet music. More sheet music is used as a journaling block at the bottom of the page. The musical symbols have been enlarged and traced on plain paper before being transferred to the black cardstock.

Digital Downloads

There is no end to the number of items you can download for free off of the Internet. When creating a page with a musical theme, look for Web sites that offer free downloads of music paper. Use them for background or for journaling.

Sonya Shaw

A Rainbow of Personality

USE COLOR TO CAPTURE THE UNIQUE ASPECTS OF YOUR CHILD'S SOUL

Color is powerful. It inspires emotion and affects physiology. That's why it is an amazing scrapbooking tool. Use color correctly, and it can tie a page together and inspire strong feelings that make viewers feel connected to the page.

Children's emotions and moods can fly from passive to emotional and back to passive in a matter of minutes. It's safe to say that children have an amazing emotional range. Every point on this range is worth capturing on your scrapbook pages, and proper use of color will help you do just that.

Amber Clark

Use Vibrant Color for Vibrant Emotion

Bright, saturated color palettes jump out, grab a reader's attention and say, "Hey! Look at me!" Brilliant neons, rich and luscious hues, happy sherbets are all excellent choices for showcasing personality. Here, the artist tempers a strong color combination with heavy and dark inked edges. She also converted the photo to black-and-white, which helps it contrast against the joyful background.

Child Logic
Capturing the things your kids say is integral to showing their personalities

Kids do say the darnedest things. They also say the most thought-provoking, surprising and downright poignant things. Here are some ideas for collecting them:

Keep a journal Buy a small journal that you can fit in your purse. When your child unleashes a gem, write it down. Flip through it for scrapbook-page inspiration.

Save the homework Is your child a particularly good writer? Encourage her to share her work with you, whether it's an essay penned about her favorite tree or a book report about her favorite story. Save these Pulitzer-worthy pieces to include on your scrapbook pages.

Inspire poetry Some kids will happily write you a poem if asked. See if you can persuade your youngster to write a poem about a current scrapbooking topic, such as the family pet or recent trip to Grandma's house.

Give It to Them, in Black-and-White

Employing the artistic contrast of black and white results in versatility. Black-and-white pages can be classic or contemporary. On this page, black and white are used to underscore the fact that this little dude has a strong personality. The artist adds hints of color with typographic patterned paper that stays true to the strong lines and contrast of the color scheme.

Amber Clark

Find Serenity in Soft Palettes

Shhh. This model is taking some "me" time. The primary color, a soft blue, finds balance and charm with its brick and white color companions. A hint of rich neutrals adds creamy equilibrium. The relaxing curves of the layout's design are contrasted with the horizontal stripes of the white patterned paper.

Amber Clark

Water-Play Fun!

A HOSE, A SPRINKLER, A POOL AND TUB

Get ready for a rompin' good time when kids meet water. Whether locked and loaded with a sprinkler or squirt gun, or dashing through a spray of water, kids are in their element. These fun-time photos of water play are equally fun to scrapbook with bright and hot sunny palettes or cool watery palettes. So dry off your munchkin and sit down to have a good time of your own.

Tina Freeman
Photos: Roxanne Schultz

Girl Power

Watch out! This girl's got a loaded hose, and she's not afraid to use it! Photos of this little squirt are mounted on a colorful platform of layered patterned papers. The stamped title is all mixed up, as though created while the artist was dodging water. Ribbons and rub-on words finish off the playful layout.

Make the Most of Your Photos

Don't get caught in a color rut thinking that all of your "girl" photos need to be scrapbooked on pastel pages! Find papers that capture the mood of the activity, the season and the colors of your girl's clothing.

Splash

Blue is the color of water, of this child's swimsuit and some types of flowers. But GREEN is the color that pops on this playful page. The green inner tube and several tiny green flowers give the page its pow factor. Layered patterned papers are bold enough to compete with the heavy-hitting green elements.

Leah Zion

Wet

This pup is wet behind the ears—and just about every place else, thanks to some sprinkler rompin' fun. The large chipboard letter title holds down an upper corner of the layout, balanced by the journaling block below. The water splashes are actually distressed flower rub-ons.

HAYDEN THE ANIMATION AND EXPRESSIONS ON YOUR FACE REFLECT YOUR RELIEF ON A HOT SUMMER DAY. THE POOL WAS NOT UP YET, SO THE LAWN SPRINKLER SERVED AS AN ALTERNATIVE. YOU RAN AND JUMPED AND PLAYED ALL AFTERNOON.

Mary Rogers

Sports Fun!

RUNNING, KICKING AND SCORING...

Watching your child in full throttle run or scanning the sky for that pop fly, you can almost imagine that gold medal around her neck. But whether your child's athletic pursuits take her to the Olympics or just down the block to the local park, they will help her grow a strong body and mind. Scrapbook the exertion of your child's sporting activities on pages that take advantage of sports-themed papers and creative journaling.

Trish Adams

Kick It Like a Girl

Torn and layered sports-themed patterned papers create a field for these terrific motion photos. This young athlete's personal philosophy is detailed in the journaling to the left of the center photo. Die cuts and stickers are used to help create the title.

Make the Most of Your Photos

Detail shots are just as important as focal photos. When photographing an event, seek opportunities to get in close and capture details. What is your child holding? What is he using to build a mud house? What are the most important pieces of the sports uniform?

Being 12

Having a 12-year-old son can keep a mother busy. So taking photos of that boy and scrapbooking them on quick and easy pages is a must! This layout mixes a black-and-white photo with a color image to achieve terrific success. The images are matted and then mounted on top of paper strips and a large circle of patterned paper. A journaling block and rub-on title words are embellished with rustic brads.

Amy Dyckovsky

Tough

A monochromatic page like this one can be overlooked if the photo isn't strong enough to carry the emotion. Luckily, this one is dynamic. The photo is scrapbooked on a patterned paper background. The heavyweight chipboard title is mounted directly on the photo, and individual letters are turned various ways for extra interest. The ribbon separates the photo from the lower portion of the page.

Beth Root

Quiet-Time Fun!

READ, DREAM AND BUILD

Shhh, children at quiet time and rest! Like adults, children need down time. Photograph their quiet moments without infringing on their activities by covertly snapping photos. Scrapbook these images to remind you that, when you've just about given up on keeping pace with your young ball of energy, nap time is just around the corner.

Sonya Shaw

Add Definition

Use a black fine-tipped marker to draw a dark edge around your title letters. This helps them visually move forward and separates them from the business of other page elements.

Mesmerize

This page is all about color, from the vibrant sunset shades in the mural to the background papers and die-cut title letters. The boy's red hair adds just another shot of heat to the layout. The calming white cardstock of the journaling block provides a resting place for the eyes. Stickers dance along the vertical borders of the page. A few small ribbons add dimension.

Firm Foundation

It takes a steady hand to build a structure as delicate as this, but this child has it all under control. Photos of his activity are scrapbooked on patterned paper overlaid by a clock transparency. Stamped numbers and letters, a circular accent and a clip from a floppy disk embellish the page. Journaling begins, "Architect? Inventor? Civil engineer? I love to look into the future, Alexander, and wonder what you'll be when you're grown."

Judith Mara

Sleep

Shhhhh. You don't want to wake this little princess! The photo of her deep in slumber is showcased on layered and stitched patterned papers in gentle earth-tone shades. Cardstock stickers and tags complete the layout.

Tristann Graves
Photo: Lance Freehofer

Art Fun!

PAINTS, CLAY AND CRAYONS

It's gonna be messy any time a child and art supplies get up close and personal. And the results of those glorious messes are sure to be coveted by parents and grandparents alike. Photograph images of artful messes as well as the final master-pieces. Journaling can be as extensive as a mural or as simple as a line drawing.

Maria Burke

Only Young Once

What a wonderful mess! This young girl's pleasure in finger (or, perhaps, body) painting makes you want to join the fun. The photos of her activity are scrapbooked on layered patterned papers. Iron-on velvet letters form the title. A metal word accent is tied with a strip of ribbon. The journaling blocks include the artist's confession that she encouraged the creative chaos by allowing her daughter to attempt to paint her own nails—with finger paints!

Spin Art

"During" and "after" pictures are colorful and powerful enough to require little visual support on this unique layout. The title letters are chipboard stickers.

Make the Most of Your Photos

Digital photo-tinting creates an avant-garde look on the "Spin" layout. Using image-editing software, open the color image, duplicate it and convert the duplicate to black-and-white. Layer the black-and-white image on top of the color image and use the eraser tool to remove the black-and-white image, allowing the color image to show through where desired.

Celeste Smith

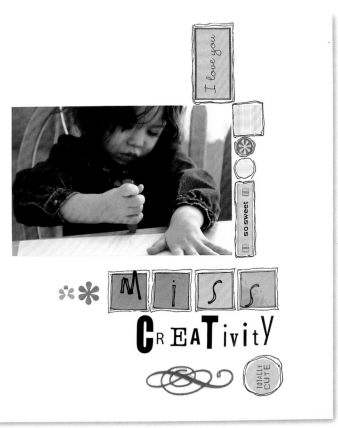

Miss Creativity

A clean white background forms the perfect palette for photos of this little artist hard at work. Stickers and pen work are used to create the title, journaling and embellishments.

Kim Musgrove

Glow

This doodle toy provides hours of fun for this youngster and provides her mother with a terrific photo opportunity. The image is scrapbooked on a simple page with rickrack, flowers and a journaling block.

Make the Most of Your Photos

With all the glorious papers and embellishments available to scrapbookers today, it takes restraint not to add a little bit of this and a lotta bit of that to your layouts. But consider occasionally fighting the desire to adorn with abandon. Clean white space results in a tranquil and emotionally compelling layout.

Amy Brown

Mini Masterpieces

WAYS TO COMMEMORATE AND PRESERVE YOUR CHILD'S ARTWORK

Excelling in art class today, taking the contemporary art world by storm tomorrow. Parents feel enormous pride in their child's early art pieces, realizing that art is a tool for creative expression. Nourish your child's artistic talents by honoring his work on your scrapbook pages.

Scrapbooking your child's artwork allows you to display the piece within a context. In the journaling, you can include such important facts as your child's age, the media used and what inspired the piece.

Samantha Walker

Frame Reduced Images

Think of a scrapbook page as a mini art-gallery wall. For this digital layout, the artist scanned and reduced three wonderful drawings by the young artist pictured. She then placed them under digital frames, creating a lovely border along the bottom of the page. For the journaling, she interviewed the artist, asking her about her favorite things to draw, favorite medium to draw with and favorite artist. To re-create this look for a traditional scrapbook page, simply print the scanned and reduced pieces and place under handmade or premade frames.

Scrapbook With Your Kids
Fun scrapbooking projects to complete with your kids that will inspire their inner artists

Fuel your child's creativity by having him participate in your scrapbooking. It's a great way to spend quality time with your child and will also give you tons of inspiration for your scrapbook pages.

Polymer clay accents Clay is a childhood favorite! Kids love squishing and molding it between their fingers. Help them create page accents with polymer clay. If they mess up, they can simply roll it up and start over.

Custom background paper Children + pens + cardstock = awesome background paper. Pick three colors that complement the photos you wish to scrapbook. Show the photos to your kids and see what emerges.

Mini scrapbook pages Dig into your paper scraps. Surely there are scraps big enough for mini scrapbook pages. Help your child pick photos, write journaling and choose accents.

Samantha Walker

Create Patterned Paper

Any piece of your child's art can be used to create patterned paper. All you need is a scanner. This paper was created by scanning two renderings of a car, which were drawn by the model in the photograph. The page artist colorized one of the cars in several hues and then created a repeating pattern. The new background paper provided the foundation for this digital page. For a paper scrapbook page, simply print the image onto acid- and lignin-free paper.

Use to Accent

Childhood artwork was used to create the title as well as a border for this scrapbook page. The artist found a stash of her husband's elementary-school artwork. She picked three drawings, scanned them and then used them to create the title. In a word-processing program, she typed the word "art" at a large point size in an outline font. She then imported the images so they would fill in the outline. The artist also was moved by a series of self-portraits her husband created that showed his physical and developmental growth. She scanned and reduced those pieces to use as a border.

Samantha Walker
Photos: Rita Walker

Goofin' Around!

BIKES, BOUNCE AND RUNNING AMUCK

There's nothing more fun than unorganized free time. Just hand your child a few hours of this commodity and he'll find a thousand ways to entertain himself. Your "goofin' around" photos will be so diverse that you'll be challenged to create innovative page designs to embrace the activities. Have fun scrapbooking your child's unstructured play in your own downtime.

Leah Zion

King of the Back Yard

It sure is good to be the king! The artist began scrapbooking this fun image with a white background and added the photo to the right side of the page. To create the funky frame, cut a piece of patterned paper into strips and then cut it into blocks. Layer the pieces around the photo in a random fashion and add machine stitching to help define the photo edges.

Make the Most of Your Photos

What good is a focal photo, or any photo on a scrapbook page, if it gets lost in the background? Make your photo pop off the page with a photo mat that contrasts against the background. It can be as simple as a thin white mat edge or photo border set against almost any type of background. Light always pops against dark. Contrast also can be achieved with a funky texture, such as frayed canvas or embossed cardstock.

Forever Young

Neatly stitched strips of patterned papers form a visual platform for this happy-go-lucky photo. Rub-on words are applied directly to the photo. Tiny decorative brads hold down the lower right corner of the page.

Kim Hughes

Whirlpool of Silliness

Remember making paper pinwheels as a child? You'd spend hours blowing on them just to see them spin. This page features one of those twirly toys on a background of stitched and layered circular papers. Another pinwheel embellishes the title, which rests below the three photos. The title is constructed from a collection of stickers and other embellishments.

Sonya Shaw

Lessons Learned
ONE SCRAPBOOKER LEARNS THE ART OF ENHANCING FOCAL PHOTOS

In an effort to convey an overwhelming feeling of love for her children, Wendy Chang inadvertently overwhelmed the photo on the scrapbook page below. "In an attempt to salvage it, I tried to frame it with journaling," Wendy says, "but the journaling just faded into the background and only added to the busyness of the page. And, worse, the words made no sense! Overall, the layout lacks cohesion and feels very flat."

With the layout's reincarnation, Wendy created a lighter background that gives the photo prominence. She also added journaling, conveying her and her husband's love for their children.

GOOD, BUT...

Patterned paper too dark to truly complement the photo subjects' complexions.

Combination of patterns, colors and stamped words distracts from the photo.

Brown stamped word frame fades into the background and gives reader no information about the photo.

Wendy Chang

BETTER!

A lighter background is more complementary to the models' skin tones. The slight white edge around the photo contrasts against the background, helping it pop off the page.

Patterned paper is used more sparingly, making it more of an accent to the page rather than a focal point.

Short, heartfelt journaling puts the photo into context for the reader.

> To our dearest children,
>
> May you always know how much you are cherished by us. We will always love you, no matter what.
>
> Love, Mommy and Daddy
>
> Picture taken 0805
> On the Little Engine that Could
> Filmore, California

CHERISH

Wendy Chang

Be a Better Scrapbooker

Points from Wendy Chang about how to relax and just be creative.

- Never feel like you are not creative enough.
- Ignore the pressure to create everything from scratch.
- Allow yourself to have fun, experiment and make mistakes.
- Allow yourself to create simple pages, if that is what you want.
- Challenge yourself to create complex pages, if that is what you want.
- Always have goals as an artist and strive to reach them.

Ya Gotta Have Love

Love truly does make the world go around. Children (and perhaps puppies!) are the best givers and takers of love. The more love they are given, the more they extend to those around them in the form of wilted flower bouquets, sticky kisses and hand-scrawled love notes.

Scrapbook the loving moments you share with your child, the gestures he gifts to others and the heartfelt love notes on pages that need to be sealed with a kiss. When the world seems too complicated, let these pages remind you that all ya need to be happy is the love of a child.

FRIENDS and

trusted kind kindred spirits free advice be yourself | mi amigo mes amis mon amis silly goofy fun quirky

FRIEND.
GOOD.

accomplice sidekick amigo buddy gal pal playmate loyal | together lucky favorites through thick and thin sharing

NEIGHBORS

FRIENDS
we've been through
a lot together & most
of it was your fault

SILLY

Chloe, Sophie, Alexa and Reese playing outside together ... Neighbors and Friends ... June, 2005

play experience run giggle laughter faith jumpen
shine live heart together freedom learn youth share
inspire perfect laugh love enjoy challenge seek stron
mories forevers mile celebrate inspire fun true playful always

Suzy Plantamura

Brotherly Love

PIGGYBACK RIDES, GAMES OF TOSS, TAGGING ALONG

Big brothers are made to mentor younger siblings. They teach their younger brothers and sisters the ways of the world, like how to throw a ball, beg for an extra cookie and where the best hiding spots are. And in turn, younger siblings teach their older brothers and sisters responsibility and how to nurture. Capture brotherly moments in photographs, and scrapbook them to be enjoyed for years to come.

Martha Crowther

Brothers

What a quintessential image! An older brother carrying his younger sibling around on his back. Start by selecting themed patterned paper and cardstock to match. Double mat the image. Print journaling in different fonts and colors and cut it into captions. Mat the captions and adhere them to your page. Finish with preprinted accents, ribbon and a bottle cap.

Embellishments: When to Say When

There are so many wonderful scrapbooking supplies on the market these days that it is easy to get carried away when including them on your scrapbook page. Before you glue down yet another embellishment, ask yourself the following:

- Will this embellishment add color to a portion of the page that seems visually dead?
- Will this embellishment help balance an unbalanced layout?
- Will this embellishment support a theme that has not already been clearly established?
- Will this embellishment draw the eye to an important portion of the page?

My Children

This photo shows two sweet faces that a mother will remember forever and ever. The artist scrapbooked this photo, which is five-years-old, very recently. In the journaling, she details how amazed she is at her sons' growth. The page is constructed almost completely of paper. To replicate, trim coordinating papers into blocks and round corners. Layer and connect blocks with stitching. Punch circles from leftover paper and embellish the layout with ribbon, a silk flower, letter stickers, rickrack and a paper clip.

Angela Moen

Best Buddies

When brothers are also best buddies, the world seems a very special place. As noted on the journaled tag hidden behind the focal photo, these two siblings adore each other. Photos of the two boys are mounted on textured red cardstock and surrounded by rounded squares cut from coordinating patterned papers. A simple title is all that is necessary to complete the sterling layout.

Nancy Kliewer

Sisterly Love

GIGGLING, NURTURING, SHARING

It is said that nothing, not even a mister, should come between a girl and her sister! That's because the special bond between female siblings is astoundingly strong. Sisters are protectors of their younger siblings, distributing hugs when knees get scraped and an outstretched hand when streets need to be crossed. Photos of sisters show the tight bond between girls who will be each other's best friends throughout their lifetime.

Margie Oliveira

Love Family

The love these two sisters enjoy is evident in this photo. The image is matted on patterned paper that proves that the right shade of purple can be called an earth tone (think of the mountains at sunset). The stamped title is joined with tiny metal letter squares, but it is the decorative beaded heart embellishment that draws the eye. It opens to reveal hidden journaling.

Miranda Ferski

Sisters

Oh MY! This page has it all, from the mass of green and pink layered patterned papers to the stitching and lovely flower embellishments. Tidy crisscross stitches connect paper elements. More stitching borders the paper title slips. Ribbons and flowery embellishments appear across the page. Large stencil letters, flowers, brads, journaling strips and rub-ons complete the layout.

Sisters Always

Button, button, who's got a button? This page does! And more than just one. Buttons adorn the corner of the photo and the frame below. They join multiple blocks of patterned papers and bits of ribbon to create geometric patterns on the red cardstock background. A journaling block shares the feelings of the artist (the girls' aunt) about the closeness her little models share.

Make the Most of Your Photos

"Red" comes in more shades than just Fire Engine. And each shade has its own emotional and visual impact that will affect your photos. When you've decided that red is going to be a part of your page palette, don't just reach for the top paper in your red stack. Deeper reds are earthy and will recede, brighter reds will scream and call the eye. Choose wisely.

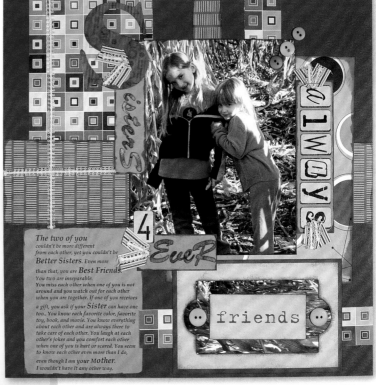

Patty Roberts

A Few of Their Favorite Things

PAGES THAT FOCUS ON THE THINGS THAT BRING YOUR CHILD COMFORT AND JOY

PB & J with the crusts cut off. A cherished stuffed animal. Trips to the park on Saturday mornings. A mother's embrace. These are just a few of the things that bring most any child both comfort and joy. They are essential to happy childhoods and therefore should be an essential theme when scrapbooking your child's life.

The next time you are inspired to make portraits or simply snap a few quick photos of your child, suggest he hold a favorite object. These honest photos will remain favorites long after the lovey has been retired.

Extended Family

Images of a young girl and her cuddly toys will be forever treasured. The artist took advantage of natural light streaming through a nearby window to light these adorable portraits. These images are mounted in opposing corners of a clean and uncluttered layout. Simply add a journaling block, a title strip and mirrored paper "E" as the only embellishment.

Alana Reeves

Still-Life Photography
Composition and lighting tips for photographing your child's favorite things

Photographing your child with his favorite object will help him relax for a photo shoot. It's also a great idea to photograph the item on its own, so all of its detail and charm will be preserved for posterity.

Understand Minimum Focusing Distance Your camera's minimum focusing distance is the distance necessary between the lens and photo subject in order for the camera to take a focused image.
Use a reflector A reflector will help bathe the object in light, allowing detail to emerge from any lurking shadows. A white sheet or piece of foam core can be used to reflect light.
Use a tripod To prevent a blurry image, steady your camera on a tripod.
Use the macro setting If your camera has a macro setting, use it to get extreme, sharp close-up shots.

Childhood Passions

How does your child feed her soul? Reading? Writing? Creating? Whatever it is, be sure to document it in your scrapbook. It makes for great pages and, more importantly, encourages your child to develop her passion. This page shows a child's love of art. The artist cropped in close on the focal photo to show the intensity of the child at work. Along the top and right side of the page, the artist framed detail shots under slide mounts. These photos show the young artist's favorite mediums.

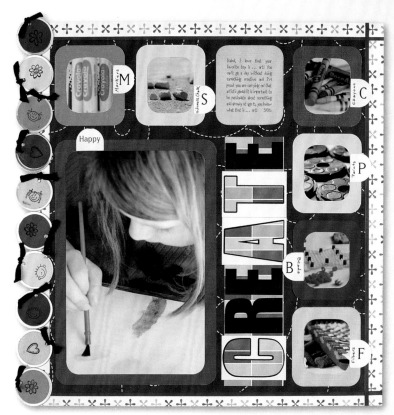

Heidi Schueller

Heidi Schueller

The Proverbial Blankie

Never underestimate the power of a blankie. It always makes a child's silver lining more obvious. This photographer caught her daughter clutching "Snuggly," her beloved security blanket. The journaling attests to the blanket's tear-curing abilities, while the soft and slightly distressed background pays homage to a well-worn comfort. The descriptive-word border details the benefits of child/blankie relationships.

Zoo Fun

ELEPHANTS, GIRAFFES AND A GOOD WALK

A trip to the zoo is as entertaining as it is educational. Children have an opportunity to stretch their legs, gawk, nibble on treats and sometimes even pet the animals! What could be better? Not much, and that's why zoo photos are so upbeat. Keep them safe on scrapbook pages that will bring back the happy memories until your next visit.

Marla Kress

Pittsburgh Zoo

How often does a child receive a deer kiss? Not often, and this artist was lucky to capture the moment in a special photo that begged to be scrapbooked. The image is mounted on a bed of patterned papers below a journaling strip. Rub-ons add a dash of color directly to the photo.

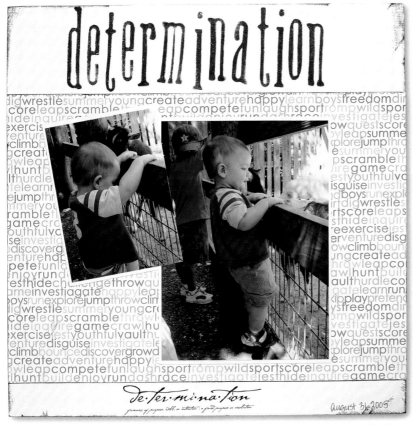

Determination

Patterned paper, stamps and rub-ons are enough to create a compelling scrapbook page without the need for more embellishments. Simply mat the photos, stamp a title and add the rub-ons to a strip of paper below. Done! Perfectly!

Valerie Wehrenberg

Beautiful

There are patterned papers for just about any page theme, but GIRAFFES?! Yes! And this super zoo page makes the most of a great print. An oversized photo featuring the majestic animal is mounted on brown cardstock. A giraffe stamp and metal disc accent embellish, while photo turns add a touch of glimmer to the photo edges. A support photo of the child and her mom are set in the lower corner of the page.

Make the Most of Your Photos

Using animal-themed papers to support your zoo photos is an excellent example of pulling pattern and texture from the images. You won't believe the number of animal-themed papers on the market today! There are spotted dog pages, lizard scale papers, furry papers, striped wildcat papers and much more! Invest in papers as you need them to support your animal-themed pages.

Randi Lanz
Photos: Ethan Lanz

Pet Love

PURRING, BARKING, SLITHERING, SCAMPERING

Pets teach children all about giving. They teach children responsibility. The bond between a child and his pet is a wonderful thing to witness. Record the special moments between them with photos. Scrapbook these tender images on pages covered with muddy paw prints or embellished with dog tags for extra fun.

Hanni Baumgardner

Lethal Cuteness

This horizontal photo of boy and dog is scrapbooked on a field of papers with gently rounded corners. No need for a journaling block when you write directly on your photo mat! And no need for extensive embellishments when the affection between boy and pet is so strong.

Make the Most of Your Photos

Children are hard enough to photograph, but add a pet into the mix and it could be a recipe for major frustration. Capture a pet's attention by using a favorite toy or treat. If it's an energetic dog you are trying to photograph, plan the photo shoot after an intense play session so the animal will be a bit more docile.

His Valentine

What could be cuter? This little boy wears his heart on his sleeve when it comes to his kitty. The enormous black-and-white photo takes over the entire page. Ribbons form frames around the image, accented in each corner with darling heart embellishments. A rub-on title and journaling block complete this loving layout.

Journaling Outside the Block

It is often easiest to journal on a designated paper block that is then mounted directly on your background paper. But once in a while you may wish to break out of the pattern and find another place to lay down your words.
Try these places:

- The back of a tag
- The edges of paper or metal embellishment shapes or directly on top of paper shapes
- A photo mat
- A slip of paper that can be tucked behind a photo and pulled out to read
- Label tape
- Ribbon or twill tape

Shannon Taylor

Heidi Schueller

Childhood "Friends"

Animals, whether live or stuffed, give children immense comfort. While girls tend to attract the fuzzy and cute, boys have a knack for all things creepy and crawly. Scales and all, these creatures were made to be memorialized in a scrapbook. This artist marvels about her nephew's intense knowledge about his pet snake, Sylvester. She mimics the slinky movements of a snake with a curving fiber accent and title alignment.

Mud Love

SQUISHY, MUCKY, WONDERFUL

Mud just makes children wanna dig in with their fingers and wiggle their toes under the cool layers. In short, WALLOW! And as a parent (who did some wallowing yourself!), you just have to let them explore the texture and enjoy the fun. Grab your camera before you even think about hosing your child down, and capture some wonderful images to scrapbook.

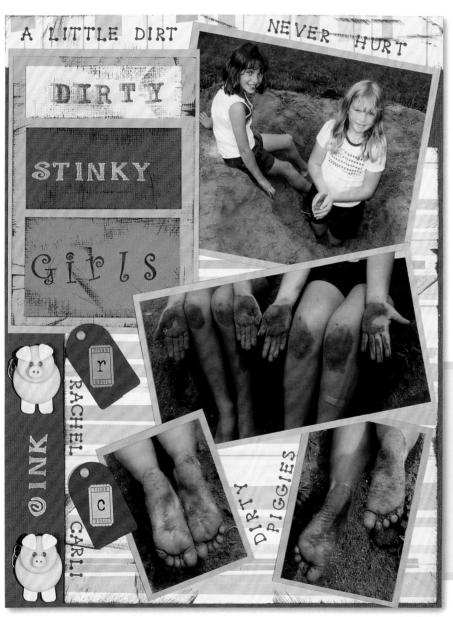

Sandy Blazek

Dirty Stinky Girls

The photos tell the story on this muddy-fun page. Photos are matted on green and orange cardstocks and mounted on striped patterned papers. The tags hold tiny raffle stickers, and tiny pig stickers poke fun at the children's pastime. You can add a bit of muddy texture to your scrapbook page with texturing paste. Apply it with your fingers, a bike tire, the bottom of a shoe or a small trowel.

Make the Most of Your Photos

When catching your kids in the proverbial act of mischievous fun, be sure to photograph all of the dirty details. Above, the artist was sure to capture the grimy feet, hands and knees.

Joy

What is it about this photo that rings of "warrior"? Perhaps it is the way this little fella seems to proudly wear his muddy war paint, or perhaps it is the slightly defiant look on his face. (His mom must be wondering why she insisted on the boots!) The quick and easy page includes a photo, ribbon and appropriate quote inside a journaling block.

Susan Merrell

I Love Mud

If mud is indeed good for a lady's skin, then this little flower is going to glow! Her fun-time experience is recorded in a terrific photo that is mounted on layered papers cut into circular shapes. A decorative flower, delicate stamped corner embellishments and ribbons holding the journaling tag remind us that this is an all-girl page.

Robbin Wood

Here We Grow!

HOW TO CREATE FANTASTIC PAGES THAT SHOW THE PASSAGE OF TIME

Remember when you were a child? It seemed as if you couldn't grow up fast enough! Now, you look at the special children in your life and wish you could hold back the hands of time. On scrapbook pages, you can! These pages show wonderful ways to capture a child's milestones.

Let these ideas inspire pages that chart physical growth. Use timelines to explain how far a child has come and where he is going. Be cognizant of the new challenges he experiences every day.

Focus on an Accomplishment

The greater the challenge, the sweeter the reward. This page explains how this little boy struggled with learning to speak. The photo shows a little boy who now never stops speaking or singing—to the glee of his parents. The artist wrapped the photo with touching handwritten journaling detailing how the challenge was met.

Marla Kress

Oh My! Another Birthday!
Fresh ideas for scrapbooking this inevitable annual event

Finding unique ways to scrapbook yearly events such as birthdays can be a creative challenge. Here are some ideas for making it a creative opportunity:

Wishes Ask the celebrant for her top five birthday wishes from the year prior and journal about which ones came true, which ones didn't and what is the outlook for the year to come.
Ask others Buy a special journal to take to the birthday party and ask guests to write a special birthday note to the guest of honor. Incorporate the notes onto scrapbook pages later.
Favorites Each year, record the birthday child's favorite things. After a few years of favorites have been gathered, create a birthday-favorites retrospective.

Capture Independence

This page conveys the bittersweet sentiment of a mother watching her toddler grow into a curious little boy. The handwritten descriptive-word journaling is supportive of his spirit, yet tugs at the heartstrings. The artist composed the photo with the subject just off-center to symbolize his forward emotional growth. A mix of energetic patterns in masculine colors adds verve.

Marla Kress

Marla Kress

Chart Facial Changes

As this artist writes in her journaling, when you live with your child day-in and day-out, you don't realize how much he grows and changes until it smacks you in the face. Here, the artist compares photos of her son at 1, 2 and 3 years old. She is beside herself with how much his facial features have changed in that time. She assures herself that despite the changes, the boy in the photos remains her same adorable baby.

Ice-Cream and Sweet-Stuff Love

WHITE CUBE FOOD GROUP

Oh yeah! Bring on the sweet stuff! Children and adults alike long for a cool cone in the summer (or just about any other time)! And when ice cream isn't on display, we'll find some other delight to introduce to our sweet tooth. Scrapbook photos of your child indulging in special treats and record the images on pages.

Ice-Cream Days

"But it has calcium, Mom!" (Not that eating ice cream on a hot day needs one, but this is a terrific excuse for a cream-covered face!) Photos are matted on pink cardstock and patterned papers. A rub-on title joins the journaling block to provide context. A candy-coated sprinkling of decorative brads finishes off the layout.

One of the best parts of summer is ice cream! Watching you devour a cone full of chocolate-chip one summer evening was just down right hilarious. You were the most focused two-year-old and you worked on that cone until there was no evidence it ever existed! What a look of satisfaction you had on your face when your task was complete, and your belly was full. Oh, happy summer days.

Holly Pittroff

Gourmet Caramel Apple

Caramel apples: YUM! Nothing more needs to be said. The photo of this boy in hog heaven is mounted on a background of earth-toned papers. Stamped and rubbed-on words and a definition sticker join journaling strips to finish off the page.

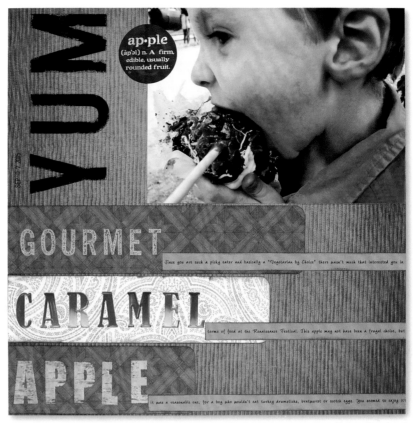

Debra Hendren

Yum

No matter how it looks, this little guy hasn't been framed—he's been caught in the act! The photo of his lollipop-eating moment, though, is indeed framed with coordinating papers. The rub-on title is also framed and tied with a decorative ribbon. Ribbons separate sections of the paper background, and a tab adds emphasis to the lower corner of the photo.

Adrienne Lehtinen

Make the Most of Your Photos

Funky frames are a guaranteed way to draw attention to your photos. In "Yum" the artist layered two contrasting yet coordinating paper frames, which she adhered over the photo so they would appear to be offset.

87

Flower Love

ROSES, DAISIES, DANDELIONS

When a child shares a flower with a parent, he is saying "I LOVE YOU!" in the loudest way he knows possible. And those wilted wildflower bouquets wilt a mother's heart. Remember your child's sweet giving nature and his awe and appreciation of nature with scrapbook pages that feature your budding son or daughter with handfuls of blossoms.

Tina Freeman

He Still Brings Me Flowers

When do children outgrow their sweet giving nature? NEVER! Moms can look forward to bouquets of wilted flowers for years! This little boy is ready to enjoy his mom's delight when he presents her with the blossom he's collected. Flower embellishments, rickrack, a journaled rub-on and a flutter of folded ribbons and game stickers support the two images.

Make the Most of Your Photos

If your page designs tend to be busy, call emphasis to the most important points in your photo by circling them with a delicate patterned paper frame. You can also purchase a metal frame, draw directly on the photo with ink or create a beaded frame by gluing micro beads to the image.

It Is the Simple Things of Life

How easy can it be to create a page? Not much easier than this! The matted photos are mounted on torn patterned paper. A torn border lines the lower edge. Journaling and two silk flowers finish the design nicely.

Amy Brown

Fun Flower Embellishments

Want a flower embellishment for your page? Use scrapbooking embellishments or silk flowers from your local hobby shop. Cut flowers from fabric patterns, use flower die cuts, brads or beads. Or create your own flower from clay!

Gwen Dye

Still Pretty

A beseeching face and handfuls of flowers sell both of these photos. Rub-on letters mounted on paper circles and a paper strip form the title. A fluffy flower with a sturdy brad embellishes the page.

Snuggle Love

HUGS, KISSES AND GENTLE SQUEEZES

Wrapping your arms around a child, you can almost hear his heartbeat align with yours. Snuggle moments are some of the best in the day. During snuggle times, the world can move on without you because you and your special little one are happily wrapped up in each other. Ask a family member to take photos of you participating in snuggle time with your child. Frame the photos or scrapbook them on warm and loving pages.

Amy McLane
Photo: Delaney Haddow

You Said

Oh, those words that popped out of our mouths when we were young! How they come back to haunt us! This delightful page is covered with journaling slips that remind this mom how different (and special) her life has become. The child in the photo is ultimate proof that she's made all the right decisions. The stamped title rests on a bed of flowers, and more flowers with jeweled centers embellish the lower page corner.

Make the Most of Your Photos

For photos that capture snuggle moments, crop in tightly. Don't let a busy background distract from the compelling image of a close bond.

Sisters

Separated by more than a handful of years,
these two sisters still share a special bond.
Photos of their interactions are matted and
mounted on layered patterned papers. The
title is spelled with clear acrylic letters and
embellished with paper flowers. A "best
friends" charm, silk flowers and photo
corners finish the layout.

Kay Rogers

Paula Gilarde

Enjoying Life

Even beautiful sunny days are more enjoyable
when you have someone with whom to share
them! These two have each other, and that's
what makes this page so special. The warm
and fuzzy photo is scrapbooked simply on
patterned papers and a light brown cardstock
background. Letter stickers are used for the
title. A leather flower embellishes the layout.
Journaling surrounds the center elements.

Rough-Housing Love
WRESTLING, GAMES OF TAG AND ROMPING

These are the moments when parents and their kids suddenly become the same age. Both are caught up in high-energy interactions that most often involve grass stains on the knees, wild giggles and even wider grins. Rough-housing times can be photographed and scrapbooked on pages that have a bit of rough and tumble texture about them. Consider ripping and distressing papers for a perfect effect.

First Love

What a Daddy's Girl you are! It was love at first sight between the two of you from the moment you arrived and if anything, that love has only grown stronger with each passing birthday you celebrate.

You can't imagine how many times Daddy looks at you and nearly tears up as he asks me, "where did my little girl go?" Though he's excited to watch you grow and learn new things, I think he worries that each new day brings you one step closer to the day you will find Love #2, the man you will choose to marry. Until that day, he's holding on to you with everything he has.

Shay Brackney

First Love

A dad holds a special place in the heart of a little girl. Scrapbook photos of your daughter enjoying daddy time on a page that is a little rough-and-tumble with torn patterned papers, distressed tags and a wood chip frame, metal letters and brads. Let the journaling tell the story of this terrific relationship.

Surrender to Your Joy

We should all remember to live life to its fullest (these two girls don't seem to need the reminder). Photos of high-powered play are featured on coordinating patterned papers. The title is created with a variety of materials, including chipboard letters, stamps, stencils and rub-ons. Perky pieces of ribbon embellish the letters.

Debbie VanMarter

Sandra Liddell

Play

Wrestling is fun! Just ask this little tyke. She's featured in a great photo beneath a jumbo paper title. Word tiles laced with blue ribbon and decorative metal brads wrap up the layout.

Make the Most of Your Photos

For a truly special photograph, get down on the level of your subjects. This is especially true when photographing children or pets.

Lessons Learned

ONE SCRAPBOOKER SHOWS HOW TO LET PHOTOS GUIDE PAGE DESIGN

It's tempting to scrapbook a trip to the beach in sepia or black-and-white to impart a serene, beachcomber mood. Samantha Walker fell into this temptation when scrapbooking the page below. The result? "I totally missed the mark on the mood and all the fun the kids were having that day," she says.

The first thing Samantha fixed about the layout was the photos. "Why in the world would I change these photos to sepia prints when the day was all about color?" she asks herself. The new version of the layout on the next page shows tons of color. Samantha really looked to the photos to inspire every aspect of the page.

GOOD, BUT...

The layout, while organized, balanced and clean, lacks a strong focal point.

The color palette is drab and doesn't convey the carefree energy of the photos.

The journaling is minimal, so the reader has no idea who the photo subjects are or how much fun they had.

Samantha Walker

BETTER!

Hello, color! The layout sparkles with vibrant, sunny energy that supports the photos.

The fun journaling invites the reader to enjoy the memory of the footloose day.

Splash!
Giggle…giggle…snort!
"Hey, who threw that mud?"

That's just one of the things I love to hear when watching my nieces and nephews play up at Bear Lake… and that's when you know… that the fun is just beginning! Those kids are so imaginative in their play…from slinging mud, to building palaces in the sand… to chasing seagulls with crackers hanging out of their mouths (um…yup…the kids mouths) hoping that they might get a close encounter of the bird kind. They make me want to be a kid again.

Samantha Walker

The enlarged photo creates a definite focal point that attracts the eye.

Be a Better Scrapbooker

8 Questions Samantha Walker always asks herself when evaluating her layouts:

- Does the page evoke the mood of the event?
- Does the page have a distinct focal point that immediately draws the eye?
- Is the viewer's eye able to travel through the page effortlessly?
- Do the photos represent the event or moment well?
- Are the photos the main focus?
- Does the journaling tell the story?
- Does it engage the reader and set a tone for the page?
- Is there color harmony, and do the colors support the theme?

Index